# Saving Our
# Animal Friends

by Susan McGrath

A little girl feeds geese and other birds beside a lake.

BOOKS FOR YOUNG EXPLORERS
NATIONAL GEOGRAPHIC SOCIETY

Have you ever held a frog in your hand? You may see frogs, insects, birds, and other creatures near your home or your school. You share your world with many wild animals.

Can you name these animals?
You won't find them in your
neighborhood. A zoo is the only place
most of us will ever see a panda
or an elephant or a tiger.

At the zoo, we can learn about such
animals. They are well cared for and
have plenty of food to eat.

A zoo worker helps a tiger cub drink
from a bottle because the mother tiger
could not feed it. Veterinarians help
keep the animals well and take care
of them when they are sick.

At a wild animal hospital, a veterinarian looks at a hawk's broken leg. His helper gently holds the bird still. The doctor also checks a squirrel that has lost its parents. The squirrel will be set free when it is older.

Many people are working hard to save wild animals. Why do they need help? In places where they live close to people, wild animals may have a hard time finding food and a safe place to live.

A fence stops a pronghorn from moving about in the snow. Animals that need large open spaces to run in get in trouble when people build fences and houses in wild lands.

Many elk live in the mountains of the West. In winter, they go down to the valleys. Today, they may find houses instead of grassland. An elk may come right up to a house, looking for food. People have set aside open land where they put out food for these animals. Without this help, many of the elk would die.

The manatee needs help, too. This large mammal lives in warm waters in Florida. It must come to the surface of the water to breathe. Motorboats zooming past sometimes hit manatees and hurt them. But people are working to protect these gentle animals.

In some places where manatees live, no motorboats are allowed. In others, signs warn people in boats to look out for manatees. You can call a special phone number if you see an injured manatee.

The place where an animal lives and finds food is called its habitat. The best way to help an animal is to protect its habitat.

We have saved many habitats in large parks and in areas called refuges. Visitors can come to these places to see the animals and learn about them. Have you ever been to a wildlife refuge?

Experts take care of the deer and birds and other animals here. Refuges also make safe resting places for birds that migrate. Canada geese and other birds stop here on their way to and from their nesting grounds.

The nesting grounds of some kinds of birds need even more protection. You are not allowed to visit them.

15

Birds called terns lay their eggs on beaches, right out in the open. What would happen if visitors walked on this beach? The birds would fly away and leave their eggs unprotected.

A mother tern sits close to her new chick. Later, both parents bring small fish for the young to eat.

Sea turtles live in the ocean. The females come to the beach to lay their eggs in the sand. The eggs are in danger on some beaches. Animals may eat them.

People have learned ways to help save sea turtles. These children are digging up the eggs to keep them safe.

When the little turtles have hatched, the children will let them crawl into the sea to grow up.

The tall white bird is a whooping crane. The darker birds are sandhill cranes. Very few whooping cranes are alive today.

A pair of whooping cranes raises only one chick each year. When scientists find nests with more than one egg, they put the extra eggs into sandhill crane nests. Sandhill cranes hatch the eggs and raise the chicks. So, many more whooping cranes live to grow up in the wild.

Once, people killed so many alligators to make purses and shoes from their skins that the animals almost became extinct. Now, laws protect alligators, and they are common again in some places. How many babies can you count resting on this mother alligator's head?

Too much hunting almost killed off the great whales. Then people made laws to protect them. Now, whales are safer. But many wild animals and their habitats are still in trouble.

Have you ever seen ugly piles of trash in the woods or by the side of the road? Trash isn't just ugly. It can injure animals.

This fox may cut itself on the sharp edges of a rusty can. The gull may be hurt by a plastic can holder caught on its head.

To help animals, we must take good care of their habitats. You can help. Always throw your trash in a trash can.

What else can you do to help save animals? Learn more about them! These children are getting to know a tame wolf. They sit quietly and watch as the teacher tells them about wolves.

Are there birds in your neighborhood? Make them a bird feeder. You can use pie pans, wire, and an empty can. Keep the can filled with birdseed all winter. The birds will depend on you.

Pinecones stuffed with peanut butter and seeds offer another treat for the birds. You can hang your feeders from a tree.

Animals need water as well as food. To give birds a drink, put out a pan of water. You may also see a bird take a bath.

A fluffy squirrel nibbles corn it found at a feeder.
Other wild animals are not so lucky. Many are in trouble.
They all need friends. Are you the animals' friend?

Someone built this house just for bluebirds.
Because other birds take their natural nesting
places, bluebirds need this kind of help.

COVER: The mountain lion, a wild cat
once common in the United States,
now lives mainly in western mountains.

Published by
The National Geographic Society, Washington, D. C.
Gilbert M. Grosvenor, *President*
Melvin M. Payne, *Chairman of the Board*
Owen R. Anderson, *Executive Vice President*
Robert L. Breeden, *Senior Vice President,
   Publications and Educational Media*

Prepared by
The Special Publications Division
Donald J. Crump, *Director*
Philip B. Silcott, *Associate Director*
Bonnie S. Lawrence, *Assistant Director*

Staff for this book
Jane H. Buxton, *Managing Editor*
Charles E. Herron, *Picture Editor*
Marianne R. Koszorus, *Art Director*
Elizabeth W. Fisher, *Researcher*
Artemis S. Lampathakis, *Illustrations Assistant*
Mary Frances Brennan, Vicki L. Broom, Carol R. Curtis, Mary Elizabeth Davis, Rosamund Garner,
   Virginia W. Hannasch, Ann E. Newman, Cleo E. Petroff, Stuart E. Pfitzinger, Virginia A. Williams, *Staff Assistants*

Engraving, Printing, and Product Manufacture
Robert W. Messer, *Manager*
David V. Showers, *Production Manager*
George J. Zeller, Jr., *Production Project Manager*
Gregory Storer, *Senior Assistant Production Manager*
Mark R. Dunlevy, *Assistant Production Manager*
Timothy H. Ewing, *Production Assistant*

Consultants
Dr. Lynda Bush, *Reading Consultant*
Dr. Ine Noe, *Educational Consultant*
Dr. Ronald M. Nowak, Office of Endangered Species, U. S. Fish and Wildlife Service, *Scientific Consultant*

Illustrations Credits
Steven C. Kaufman (cover); Wolfgang Kaehler (1); F. Eugene Hester (2-3); Jessie Cohen/National Zoological Park/Smithsonian Institution (4-5 all); Susan McElhinney (6, 7, 14-15 all, 28 lower, both, 29 lower, 30-31); C. C. Lockwood (8-9, 26 lower); Jeff Foott (10-11 both, 17 upper, 20 left); Fred Bavendam/PETER ARNOLD, INC. (12); Jeff Foott/TOM STACK & ASSOCIATES (13); ANIMALS ANIMALS/Allan Rokach (16 upper); Wendell D. Metzen/BRUCE COLEMAN INC. (16-17 lower); Ian Howarth (18); Paul A. Zahl (19 upper); Frans Lanting (19 lower); G. C. Kelley/TOM STACK & ASSOCIATES (20-21); John Cancalosi/TOM STACK & ASSOCIATES (22-23 upper); Townsend P. Dickinson/NAT'L AUDUBON SOCIETY COLLECTION/PR (22-23 lower); Flip Nicklin/NICKLIN & ASSOCIATES (24-25); Tom J. Ulrich (26 upper); Keith H. Murakami/TOM STACK & ASSOCIATES (27); National Geographic Photographer Joseph H. Bailey (28-29 upper); Robert C. Simpson (32).

**Library of Congress CIP Data**
McGrath, Susan, 1955—
   Saving our animal friends.

   (Books for young explorers)
   Summary: Describes ways people help some wild animals in need of human
protection, particularly in keeping their environments safe for them to live without injury.
   1. Wildlife conservation—Juvenile literature. [1. Wildlife conservation] I. Title. II. Series.
QL83.M35 1986                    333.95'416                    86-5177
ISBN 0-87044-635-5 (regular edition)
ISBN 0-87044-640-1 (library edition)

# MORE ABOUT

## Saving Our Animal Friends

**W**hy do we care about wildlife? Different people might offer different reasons. But perhaps the most fundamental reason is this: the tremendous diversity of life on earth adds richness to our lives that cannot be replaced.

Why are so many animals in trouble? Their most serious problem is loss of habitat. Wild animals share the earth with humans and must compete with them for space. Most often, the animals are the losers.

How do animals lose their habitat? The land is developed—drained, filled, and farmed or built upon. Some animals, such as raccoons, opossums, and many kinds of birds, adapt to the new conditions. But most animals do not survive.

Pollution—pesticides, oil spills, toxic wastes, and garbage—can make any area unfit for animals to live in. Even litter can be dangerous. Plastic six-pack holders can strangle. Metal flip-tops can injure (26-27).*

Too much hunting and exploitation have brought some species to the verge of extinction. For example, **whales** (24-25) were hunted for their fat, which was made into oil for lamps, for cooking, and for use as industrial lubricants. Whales were also killed for their baleen, which was used in making corsets and buggy whips. **Alligators** (22-23) were sought by the leather industry for their unusual hides. Live parrots, other birds, and mammals were caught to be sold as exotic pets.

In 1903, President Theodore Roosevelt signed an order making Florida's Pelican Island the country's first national wildlife refuge. Since then, more than 400 refuges have been set aside—ranging from less than an acre at Minnesota's Mille Lacs to 20 million acres at Alaska's Yukon Delta. On this map, silhouettes of Canada geese in flight mark the location of those refuges in the lower 48 states that allow visitors. Is there one near you? Visit it!

*Numbers in parentheses refer to pages in *Saving Our Animal Friends*.

The illegal hunting continues, but laws now control both capture and killing of wildlife in most countries. As a result, some species are recovering. Alligators, hunted to near extinction 20 years ago, have so recovered that some states allow controlled hunting. Great whales—blues, humpbacks, and others that have been hunted extensively—are now protected by an international ban on commercial whaling.

Though some people regret seeing any animal killed, regulated hunting can benefit wild animal populations. Natural predators, such as wolves and bobcats, have been killed because people considered them destructive pests. In the absence of predators, populations of prey species such as deer can grow rapidly, upsetting the natural balance of an area. The animals begin to starve. Hunting helps keep their numbers under control.

Hunting helps in another way, too. Waterfowl hunters over the age of 15 must buy Duck Stamps issued by the U.S. Fish and Wildlife Service every year. Proceeds from these stamps go to buy new acres of wetland refuge. Many non-hunters buy the stamps, too, as a contribution to conservation.

Refuges assure many wild animals of places to live (14-15). But in some cases, wild species are in such trouble that a safe habitat alone will not ensure their survival. Whooping cranes (20-21), for instance, would probably not exist without human help. Wildlife managers have created a foster-parent program: They use a flock of sandhill cranes, a more numerous species, to help hatch and raise the whooping crane young.

By doing this, experts hope to create a second flock of whooping cranes. The original wild flock migrates from Texas to northern Canada every year. The trip is long and full of dangers. It is hoped that the whooping cranes raised by sandhill cranes will start a new flock that will migrate between New Mexico and Idaho, as their foster parents do.

Like whooping cranes, certain sea turtle species need active management if their populations are to recover. A female sea turtle lays dozens of eggs in a nest on the beach, but many of the nests are destroyed. And of the turtles that hatch, only a few reach maturity. Volunteers in the coastal states, Costa Rica, Caribbean islands, and other areas of the world help by guarding turtle nests. Special permits allow some of these volunteers to remove eggs from the sand and hatch them in incubators (18-19).

Though many animals need help, misguided animal lovers sometimes do more harm than good. It is best never to handle wild animals; but if you must, learn how to handle them properly. For example, be careful when you pick up a frog. You can injure it if you hold it too tightly. Return any animal to its home after you have examined it.

If you see a baby animal alone, do not assume it is orphaned. Call for help before making a rescue attempt that may only hurt the animal. Your local Humane Society, SPCA, veterinarian, or game warden can recommend a licensed wildlife rehabilitator to call for advice.

In Florida, the Marine Patrol monitors boat traffic to protect manatees (12-13) and maintains a marine animal hotline number. If you ever see a manatee in trouble, you can report it to the patrol promptly.

In what other ways can you become involved in the struggle to save wildlife? Find out what species in your area are in trouble. How can you help them?

Are there **bluebirds** in your neighborhood? Build them nesting boxes like the one on page 32. Is there litter in a park or streambed near your house? Mobilize a group of friends, young and old, with gloves and garbage bags, and clean it up!

Visiting wildlife refuges can be an interesting way to learn more about animals and plants. Refuges offer seasonal havens to millions of birds that migrate north and south every year. They also provide permanent homes for fish and other wildlife, including endangered species such as the bald eagle.

Experts offer these practical tips for visiting refuges:
● Contact the personnel at a refuge before visiting. They can offer directions and valuable advice.
● Check in at the visitor center as soon as you arrive.
● Dress comfortably for the season. Wear sturdy walking shoes or boots.
● Bring binoculars and wildlife identification guidebooks.
● Respect the wildlife you came to see—speak quietly, be careful not to startle the animals, and watch where you step.

## ADDITIONAL READING

*Alligators, Raccoons, and Other Survivors,* by Barbara Ford. (N.Y., William Morrow, 1981). Ages 10-12.

*Animals in Danger.* (Wash., D.C., National Geographic Soc., 1978). Ages 4-8.

*Endangered Animals,* by Dean Morris. (Milwaukee, Raintree, 1977). Ages 5-9.

*Wild Lands for Wildlife,* by Noel Grove. (Wash., D.C., National Geographic Soc., 1984). Family reading.

*Wildlife Alert!* by Gene S. Stuart. (Wash., D.C., National Geographic Soc., 1980). Ages 8-12.